SEEING GOD

IN

HIS CREATION

POEMS

ELIZABETH BRUCE
&
ELIZABETH TOMLINSON

'For since the creation of the world God's invisible qualities ---
His eternal power and divine nature --- have been clearly seen,
being understood from what has been made, so that men are
without excuse.'

Romans 1.20 The N.I.V Bible

POEMS

ELIZABETH BRUCE

The Path Of Peace

There is a path where roses bloom,
Where sky is blue and air is warm,
And on that path I'll walk with you.
Come, walk with Me!

Come walk with Me and know My peace,
In spirit find your true release.
My pathway leads to views unknown.
Come, trust in Me!

Come trust in Me though the way is long,
But you will sing a triumph song
Along the path that you must go
If you love Me!

If you love Me then walk with Me.
Where my way leads the heart is free,
And you'll find rest to refresh your soul.
And know My peace!

Garden Of Holiness

I walk in the garden of holiness
When the cares of my day have begun,
And commune with the Son of all righteousness,
Our spirits united as one.

His Word as refreshing as dew drops
That rest in the heart of the rose;
His voice as the whispering of breezes
That murmur in the trees at days close.

The peace of His Presence surrounds me
As a mantle when evening draws nigh;
The perfume in His garden over powers me
With a fragrance I cannot deny.

His blossoms that bloom in abundance
Are gentleness, mercy and love,
And the fountains and stream-lets that wander
Quench my thirst for His mansions above!

If this is a glimpse into heaven,
His garden beyond all compare,
Then my future is safe in His keeping
Fore ever to walk with Him there!

Come, walk in the garden of holiness
When the cares of your day overcome,
And commune with the Son of all righteousness,
Your spirits united as one!

****

His Glory

The workings of the Universe I do not understand,
All of it created by mighty powerful hands!

I do not know how birds can fly, or why the willow bends.
All of nature's mysteries I cannot comprehend.

My mind cannot imagine how high the mountains raise,
As if they stretch towards the sky to offer God their praise!

I only know that Jesus was born and died for me,
And by His holy sacrifice new pastures I will see!

But there is one stipulation of which I am aware.
Obedience to acknowledge that Christ my Lord is there!

His Cross

God can make a rosebud,
Perfection unadorned!
God can paint a sunrise
At every break of dawn!
He can turn a wilderness
Into a garden fair,
But He cannot make a sinner
Into a saint, unless they care!

He controls the ocean,
Brings seasons changing scenes.
He understands our feelings
And knows what suffering means.
Mighty are His miracles
And nothing is for loss,
Yet He can't make saints from sinners
Until they accept Christ's cross!

Mounting High

An eagle is born to fly above in realms of liberty,
Soaring to heights of sheerest joy in situations free!
Floating upon the crystal air beneath a turquoise sky,
Resting upon the highest crag to watch the world go by!

But:

An eagle reared in captivity never learns to fly.
The powerful wings cannot know the joy of rising high!
And so this bird who was designed to scale the heights of heaven,
Is forced to live a stinted life not using pinions given!

We too are as the eagle born. We too were born to fly!

But:

When we remain a captive we hunger waste and die.
Because we're not fulfilling our part in God's great plan,
He wants us all to understand the freedom given to man!

It is so very easy to unlock our cage and fly,
To find our wings and rise above into the crystal sky!
To know the joy of soaring in situations free,
Being at One with Jesus the Lord of liberty!
To know His power manifest in the heart of life's dark storm,
Knowing His hour of victory even when the shadows loom!

All we need do is open the door into our heart,
And ask Him to release us into a world apart,
By seeking His forgiveness and repenting of the past,
So finding life's fulfilment in precious things that last!
Then we know the wonder and the freedom given to man,
Mounting on eagle's wings in obedience to God's plan!

****

Patch Of Blue

Sometimes from my window view I sit and watch the sky.
My personal little patch of blue that no one sees but I!
Different shades I witness according to the day,
And there are pictures high above when clouds are holding sway.

Layer upon layer moving fast and moving free,
But sometimes they linger and hide the blue from me.
Yet in their shape and shadow there is so much to see,
Private secret pictures no one understands but me!

Life is like my window view and no one knows but I
The many little personal things that come to cloud my sky!
Different shades of living make up each separate day,
But God is my contentment however dull the way!

Layer upon layer of trouble's come and go
And how to overcome them He alone does know!
He always has the answer and it's Him who clears my sky,
To give my own small patch of blue that I cannot deny!

Treasure Chest

We need no gold or precious stones to make our life complete.
No velvet gown to wrap around or carpet beneath our feet!

For we have gold enough to spare in sunset gleaming bright,
And jewels to shine and light our way on high in sky at night!

A mantle rich of Love surrounds wherever we may roam,
And heaven's way is soft to tread. Rich carpet leading Home!

All worldly riches cannot last, when comes our time to go
Possessions we must leave behind, but Love's true mercy's flow

And give to us a treasure chest that waits through heaven's door!
Why crave for fading worldly things when God's reward is sure?

God's Creation

What can be said about God's Creation?
We all see His wonders with different eyes!
The painter may seek after light and shadow,
The poet sees beauty in hidden disguise!
The author may glean through imagination
And store away scenes in recesses of mind.
Others may linger and capture creation
Just standing amazed at God's wondrous design!

Wonderful world of God's precious blessings,
How man abuses His gifts to mankind!
Life that is given to enhance with protection
As seasons revolve leaving memories behind!
For man was fashioned to tend and rule over
The beautiful place that God made on earth,
Yet how can he appreciate his given calling,
Until his experience of spiritual re-birth?

In Memory Alone

Could I but paint a picture of the beauty that I see,
And capture upon canvas the details of the sky
That changes every moment, like waves upon the sea,
Never waiting ever moving unrestricted by the eye!

Could I but capture colour that reveals itself at night.
The crimson shaded layers as the sunlight slips away,
And the majesty of storm clouds gilded by ethereal light,
Like a fire in the heavens as we lose another day!

As I watch the panorama there before my gaze,
Suddenly it vanishes as if never there.
Only memories linger as by an inner haze
And the heart is left to hunger with unspoken depths of praise!

Ethereal Light

Moonlight through my window lighting up the room,
Ethereal light from heaven brightening the gloom,
Reflection of earth's great sun that shines to light our way,
Watching over all the world, that moves within its sway!

This moon that shines so brightly is the moon that Jesus saw,
Before man nailed Him to the cross and opened heaven's door!
Two thousand years of mystery, yet still the same bright orb,
Speaking to man of how his life should reflect the Son of God!

The Place Of Forever

There's a place of love and sunshine over the rim of the hill,
Where the grass is green and the air is pure and all is quiet and still.
Except for the joy of birdsong and ripple of sparkling streams
That flow through meadows and valleys, a place of beautiful dreams!
Sheep roaming quietly grazing, lambs skipping joyfully,
No harm or ill befalls them for the Shepherd cares constantly!
He tends His sheep in the sunshine of this wonderful place of love,
Where light is always shining and no shadows of night can come.
They know His voice when He calls them. He knows each one by name.
He loves them all most dearly, bought with His Blood and pain!
And they know the price of their purchase, their Shepherd they all adore,
Heeding His hand of guidance they will not alone explore!

For He knows the path they must travel, He knows every step of the way
That leads to the place of forever where it is always day!
To reach this place of beauty we must climb to the top of the hill.
Sometimes the way is stony, sometimes hard and chill.
For this side of the hill lies in shadow and we must keep in the Light
To follow the path to the top of the hill to the place that is never night!

****

God Of The Impossible

Nothing is too hard for Him who made the birds to fly,
Who caused the oceans ebb and flow put clouds up in the sky!
Nothing is too difficult for Him who brings the snow
To overrule man's efforts and His sovereign power to show!

Nothing simply nothing is impossible for God!
Read His mighty wonders written in His Word.
Why do we not trust Him for all His Word conveys?
He can take our circumstance and change our problem days.

He can meet financial needs, bring healing for the soul,
He can mend the broken heart and make the body whole!
If we will allow Him, just committing every hour
To give Him opportunity to show His mighty power!

His promises are wonderful, His faithfulness ne'er fails,
He has the answer in His hands for everything that ails.
And life proves very different when lived within His care,
He wants so much to share with us the things He has prepared.

'Oh God of the impossible, forgive our lack of faith,
That turns aside Your mighty works and leaves us in disgrace.
And change us into people who will know the joy of just
Living within Your mysteries in simple faith and trust.'

****

Longed For Peace

'Oh you of little faith, why did you doubt?'
Said Jesus to Peter. But all Peter heard was the shout
Of wind and waves,
Forgotten his witness of former days
When Jesus proved His power o'er human ways!
In Peter's testing hour faith failed.
He sank and needed help and low was laid,
But the hand of Jesus lifted and saved from watery grave!

How often we doubt when called to trust His mighty power,
Our eyes from Jesus stray.
We see the power of the storm and try in our own way
To walk on water!
Comes the day when human understanding at last sees
Our need of Him who calmed the raging seas
And caused the storm to cease. Gives longed for peace!

Mountain Of Life

Don't look at the climb on the mountain of life,
Keep your eyes on the summit view!
The way may be hard with rocks of all kinds.
But think what is waiting for you!
With eyes on God's promise of eternal life
When we climb by the path He has shown,
The hardest of lessons become stepping stones
And we find how our strength has grown!
Without life's problems we cannot learn
How to trust in the name of the Lord,
With each lesson becoming a well-meaning friend
As we rest in the truth Of God's Word!
Praising for trials that would overpower
Were it not for the Lord's loving care,
But with Him as our guide on the mountain of life
There is comfort in knowing Him there!
So look to the summit, not heeding the climb
Keeping thoughts on His wonderful way,
With blessings outnumbering all worldly concerns
As He undertakes every day!

Harvest Of Blessings

Stretched beyond limit, or so it would seem,
When pressures continue to press more and more!
We wonder can this be a nightmarish dream,
As day after day our problems soar.

Yet God has His purpose as yet unknown
And He has a reason for all He allows.
As the blacksmith must temper to strengthen the shoe
So we need God's chastening by His mighty powers!

In the heat of the fire we learn how to trust
His infinite wisdom, faithful and sure,
To come forth as gold when the process is done,
Preparing each soul for life evermore!

So do not despair when life becomes hard,
Many blessings are given to carry us through.
As nature replenishes after the storm
So God gives His harvest of blessings for you!

Reflection!

We thank You Lord for roses,
What beauty they display!
To bless the heart with gladness
When life seems cold and grey.
You made them to perfection
Blending colours with such care,
And then You gave them perfume
For everyone to share!

May our lives reveal Your beauty
As the rose in all its glory,
And the fragrance of Your Presence
Tell its own amazing story!

SPRINGTIME

ELIZABETH BRUCE

Springtime

When daffodils are dancing
And the birds increase their song,
When sunshine's touch is warmer
And days becoming long,
Then everywhere shows promise
Of the beauty yet to be.
Is nature's promise glowing
In the heart of you and me?

Finding God is springtime
His awakening of the heart!
Loving Him brings promise
That never can depart!
Knowing Him brings beauty
And joy unknown before.
Spring can come at any time
When we open our heart's door!

Heavenly Gifts

Cottage gardens bright with dancing gems,
The daffodils that grace the winter's end!
Life's refreshment after months of storm,
Miracles of loveliness to greet the morn!
Golden clusters swaying in the breeze,
Graceful harbingers, what fairer sight than these?
Heavenly gifts to cheer, delight, and give
A reason to be thankful for sight and life to live!

Hallelujahs

We see You in the trees and flowers of Springs most glorious
days.
Nature proclaims Your mighty power and the wonders of Your
ways!

In sky and vale, in sunshine's ray, as clear as spoken word,
In breezes shrill on distant hill sweet melodies are heard!

All proclaiming 'Christ is Lord and risen from the dead'
We bow before Your glory Lord as Springs swift days are shed.

So many things that speak of You. So many blessings given
That float upon the wings of time and grant a glimpse of heaven!

In primroses, anemone, in bluebells haze of blue,
In river winding, cuckoo's call, they all give praise to You!

If all creation in its splendour holds not back such praise to bring,
So we too should raise in wonder Hallelujahs to the King!

The Path Beyond

The path led through the bluebell wood, so quiet midst Springs
display.
No traffic noise to mar the joys of such a glorious day!
We sat enjoying nature's dress of iridescent blue
And wondered on the pathway winding on and out of view!

What lay beyond our mortal gaze within that wooded glade?
We'd never know unless we walked the path where squirrels
played!
And such is life. The path beyond winds on and out of sight,
With times of beauty either side to calm our mortal plight!

But we can only briefly stay to gaze upon such joys
The path beyond must be explored whatever life employs.
Each step along the way may bring it's own particular trials
Of disappointments sadness, and heartache through the miles.

Yet taking time to stop and gaze upon the tranquil scenes,
Draws us closer to the One Who knows what suffering means.
And He will take us by the hand to guide us safely on,
If we are willing for His way! He knows the path beyond!

Springs Lullaby

As Springs green mantle softly falls
O'er field and woodland, dale and hill,
And primroses are seen again
On banks of hedgerow, hearts to thrill.
We praise You Lord for this fair land
And for each gift Your love has planned!

The trees that once were cold and bare,
Black fingers raised toward the sky,
Now stand revived by sunshine's warmth,
Blossom wreathed. Springs lullaby!
We thank You Lord for nature's blessing,
Within each bloom Your love confessing!

For life anew each springtime given
Revealing truths through nature's scene.
For gifts that speak of paths to heaven
From Your eternal Majesty!
We honour Your Almighty ways
And offer all our thanks and praise!

Morning Lesson

The robin in my birdbath was having such a game,
He really was enjoying it despite the falling rain.
He comes each day to sing for me his bright and joyful song
And in his joyful melody I see where I belong.

Keeping a happy spirit no matter what the day,
Living in perfect harmony within God's Holy sway!
Accepting what He plans for me, as taught by Robin friend,
Who trusts for all he needs to live and praises without end!

The Lilac Tree

The beauty of the lilac gone
With battering winds upon
Each frail and tender bloom!
Day after day the onslaughts came
From north they blew
To make their claim,
To bend and twist causing pain
Until low each blossom strewn.

We too can know the north winds blow
Upon the life we make, to grow
Into our perfect plan!
Beauty made by human thought
Suddenly destroyed. We're caught
In pain and bruising, to be taught
The empty ways of man!

Far better to be in the sway
Of One who knows each perfect way,
Allowing Him the helm.
Then when the north winds blow
We can in confidence go
To Him Who will the answer know.
Within the higher realm!

The tree remains tho' blossoms gone,
It stands deep rooted firm and strong,
To bloom another year.
We too can stand what e'er the strife
That comes upon this finite life
If rooted in 'The Lord of Life'.
We stand and have no fear!

****

Spring Cleaning

The first warm rays of sunshine
Show up the dirt and grime,
That gathers on the windowpanes
Through winter's gloomy time!
And marks that go unnoticed
Within the warmth of home,
Show they need attention!
Spring cleaning time has come!

And thus it is with Jesus!
When His light shines upon
The darkness that destroys us
Without the Son of God!
We need His perfect cleansing
To wash away the stain
Of living life in conflict
To His Holy Name!

What feeling of refreshment
When spring cleaning time is done,
When all is fresh and sparkling
To greet the morning sun.
And thus it is when humbly
We make our peace with God,
And know the joy of living
Beneath Christ's precious Blood!

****

MEMORIES OF SUMMER

ELIZABETH BRUCE

Wanderings in the Lake District

See the towering mountains as they reach towards the sky.
White puffs of cloud formation gently passing by.
The brightness of the sunshine revealing colours rare
In the flowers of the hillside. I can only stand and stare!

See shadows on the mountains as storm clouds gather o'er.
Both frightening and menacing the mighty thunder's roar,
And yet in these grey shadows is a beauty not revealed
When bathed in sunshine's glory, such beauty is concealed!

See the highland cattle red velvet coats adorned,
At peace in their surroundings all interruption scorned.
And oh what grand perfection of lakes both deep and wide,
In stillness their reflection allies with countryside!

Hear the gentle whisper of grass as breezes bless.
Lift your face to feel the touch of nature's sweet caress.
Feel the peace of heaven and sense God's holy power
Through His grace and Presence with you in His given hour!

Jesus loved His mountains for there He could abide
In communion with His Father and refresh His human side.
We too can know this Oneness if we take the time to rest
Within the arms of Holy peace and know His quietness!

We too can know His beauty even when the storm clouds lower,
He will reveal our hidden blooms and bring them into flower,
And they will take on depths of hue we did not know was there
Until the clouds of life came down to bring us near despair!

And as the towering mountains stand unchanged by nature's
clime,
So we can stand against all odds within God's power divine,
Looking toward the mountain peak and climbing to reach our
goal,
Knowing the peace of God to keep the quietness of our soul!

He has given us a coat to wear of His most precious cloth,
It is the Calvary Blood of Christ that covers us from wroth.
And when we wear it wisely we can travel unafraid,
Content in our surroundings by the promises Christ made!

Climbing our daily mountains with hope and not despair,
Keeping our vision fixed above where the view is always fair,
Praising for God's provision, for His wondrous mighty plan,
How gracious His design of love to thrill the heart of man!

****

Busy Bee

How hard you do work sweet Honey Bee
Gathering pollen not caring for me!
Only intent upon work to be done,
Seeking each flower for day is soon gone!
Foraging deep in the heart of each one,
Up and down in and out, no time for fun!
Sharing, no squabbles enough for you all,
Buzzing and humming how pleasant your call!
Never resting, a living to earn,
Through you we humans a lesson could learn!
How peaceful it is this afternoon free
Just watching and listening to industrious bee!
Praise God for the lessons in His creation.
To benefit man whatever his station!

Fill Me

Fill me with things that are given for me!
God's loving provision that I can see.
The beauty displayed in a dew-drenched rose.
Colours that linger at sunset's close.
Perfume enhanced by a summer night
Wafting its dream of pure delight!
Meadows of gold, the sun kissed corn.
Mountain shadows at break of dawn.
The curlews call, the lark so free,
Oh fill me with things that are given for me!
Fill me with all these things that I love,
For in this way I am filled with God!

Rural Kent

The hills of Kent show clear against the sky,
And cloud formations wax and wane as they pass by!
Casting shadows across expanse of land,
Moving changing patterns controlled by mighty Hand!
Oh the wonder to gaze upon a scene of rural splendour,
A peaceful summer dream.

The distant humming of combine in the corn,
And rabbits playing white powder puffs adorned.
Late summer beauty, joys that live forever
Within a heart that is tested beyond measure!
Only God could plan such detail in His own perfect way,
Delight to give, to bless and refresh the soul
To stand and meet another day!

Gift Of Nature

What joy, a thrush was singing in the orchard o'er the wall,
I looked and saw him sitting in the branches, and his call
Was beautifully melodious in the freshness of the morn,
And all my day's anxieties just melted and were gone.

This little bird so joyful gives me pleasure every day,
He comes to this his favourite spot to sing, as if to say
'Come join me in my worship of Him who made all things,
Give Him praise and honour and taste the joy this brings.'

What joy we often forfeit when we take no time to hush
And listen to life's music that surrounds us. In the rush
To conquer daily duties that causes stress and strain,
When a pause to hear life's beauties brings instant happiness!

And it doesn't cost a penny to look around and see
The many lovely blessings God provides for you and me!
With eyes and ears open to acknowledge nature's things
We too will raise our voices to praise the King of Kings!

A Place To Rest

The garden looked so beautiful in dress of colours bright.
The lawn was trimmed and cared for with not a weed in sight.
But upon closer inspection within the flower bed
Were growing undetected weeds thought to be dead!
Weeds that bind and suffocate if left upon their own,
And having other things to do these weeds were left alone!

Looking upon the garden again when weeks had flown
Her dress of many colours was drab and overgrown,
Because the weeds had multiplied and taken all control,
Destroying all the beauty, destruction was their goal!

And so it is within our lives, if we leave weeds to grow,
The weeds of sin soon take charge and choke life's perfect flow.
It is not long before we see all beauty die away
As we are strangled by the things that lead us to dismay!
Praise God, He has the answer to cleans, and to destroy
The misery and corruption the weeds of death employ.

It is by daily meeting Him before the Throne of Grace
That we can keep life's garden a clean and holy place!
Fit for Him to walk in: and with His Presence bless!
A place of quiet beauty where we can be at rest!

****

AUTUMN GLORY

ELIZABETH BRUCE

Harvest Stored Away.

Moments to remember in a world of pain.
Quiet times of beauty given for our gain!
On a day stolen from the midst of summer's glory
Comes beauty to recapture that tells its own story.
Paths to wander,
In mind following pilgrims on their mission.
Hills to scan.
In wonder of land's tradition!
Intruding upon wildlife, enjoying nature's way.
Oh there's so much for which we need not pay!
God is good! His riches flooding everywhere,
All around His mysteries are given year on year.
As mind's harvest is once more stored away,
Moments to remember will endure through winter grey!

Life's Ploughing

The farmer ploughs to sow the seed
And reap a good reward.
The earth is churned and broken
Before he can record!
Much toil and patient waiting
He must bring to bear
Before the ripened harvest
He can joyfully declare!

So God must do His ploughing
Within the heart of man,
To bring a bounteous fruit-age
And complete His holy plan!
For until our thoughts are broken
Upon His rack of Love,
We cannot know the wonder
Of His harvest from above!

Take Time!

The glory of an autumn day
Lay fresh upon the land.
Each fold of hills and new ploughed earth
Revealed God's Mighty Hand!
A lowering sun in splendour shone
Upon this rural scene,
And gave a tired and lonely heart
Fresh hope for things unseen!
The cares and pressures of this life
Can swamp and overpower,
Unless we take the time to breathe,
If only for an hour!
To stand and gaze and think upon
The beauty God so freely,
Provides each day for everyone,
The prosperous and the needy!
His power lives, His glory hides
In things we never see,
Until we take the time to gaze
Upon His Majesty!

WINTER'S PROMISE

ELIZABETH BRUCE

A Power Of Peace

On cliff top high in December sunshine
The peace of God descended,
And all was one with Him.
Sky, sea and air, a seagulls cry,
Spoke of wonders yet seen by human eye!
A power of peace beyond man's understanding,
God's mantle wrapped His love around
And all creation hushed in adoration
Of Him who in that moment was profound!
Not mere sensation or passing glimpse of time,
But deep assurance that I am His and He is mine!
And in each other we fuse with nature's story,
For life lived for God must be united for His glory!
Not just a moment blest upon a perfect day,
But part of eternity that will forever stay!
Never again may such a moment rare return.
We need but once to taste a glimpse
Of heaven's home!

Joy To Live

When the day is cloudy with dull and lifeless hues
Remember way beyond is still an ocean depth of blues.
With warmth and rays of sunshine to cheer the longing heart,
Over-ruling darkened skies, that one day will depart!

Without the days of cloud and rain we would see no flowers grow.
Only through a testing time is there a chance to show,
How strong our faith to wait and trust for brighter days to come
Given by God's loving hand when victory has been won!

Behind the clouds of daily toil is where the Lord abides.
When we ask Him He will come and brush the clouds aside,
Filling us with joy and peace that only He can give.
Then no matter what the day how joyfully we can live!

Transformation

Beneath the hard and snow clad earth
New life awaits the spring,
And on the promise of the breeze
Fresh hope is gathering.
The first warm rays of sun dissolves
Hard winter's frosty frown,
And nature stirs with joy to be
Transformed by Springs new gown!

Beneath the surface of our being
We too have life anew,
That needs the touch of Holy Hands
To bring the beauty through!
And when we turn from winter's night
To seek the light of spring,
We rise with joy to greet God's Son
Changed by His hallowing!

Throw off the old and greet the new,
Let springtime blossoms grow.
Discard the cold of former days
Allow God's love to flow.
For He would have us rise and be
Transformed, as springtime morn.
Washed by the dews of Calvary
To know our self re-born!

****

A Winter Miracle

I saw a miracle today,
A tiny fragile gem
Of purest white simplicity
On green and slender stem!

This delicate and dainty flower
That hangs her head in shame,
Shows no pride or vanity.
She seeks no praise or fame.

Just content to quietly show
Her beauty, so fair and free,
Withstanding winter's cruellest blows
And warming hearts that see!

Could we be like the snowdrop?
Content to do our share?
In life's cold night of circumstance
May we show God's beauty there!

****

Eyes Of Love

I saw the dampness of the day and heard the chill winds blow,
No hope of washing drying or a bracing walk to go.

Then as I gazed with 'eyes of love' upon this dismal scene,
It opened up before me into joys I had not seen!

Upon the wall outside my room was hung a shawl of lace,
A cobweb clothed in misty veil the barren wall did grace.

And just beyond frail snowdrops were growing, white and pure,
Dainty heralds of the spring gave their message at my door!

And further on the golden spikes of crocus did abound,
Like candles glowing in the mist they shone from cold hard ground!

Hanging on the clothes line were diamonds gleaming bright,
Such precious jewels to grace the day and give the heart delight!

I little cared the washing lay damp and sadly by
Waiting for the sun and wind to come and blow it dry,

For I had seen the hand of God at work outside my door,
And read His message, known His love and felt His peace for
sure!

Lost within His Presence, I saw His beauty there,
Through web and flower in raindrops. A picture of His care!

He showed me that His love still clothes our dull and barren way
As mists of morning clothed the web and beautified the day.

Snowdrops revealed that I must stand unmoved in face of frost,
However hard my life may prove I should not count the cost.

And as the spikes of crocus gleamed my light must burn secure,
To show a world when dark and drear my Saviour's mighty
power!

Can any day be lacking when I seek to find the cure,
In praise and worship, giving thanks for blessings that endure?

****

Jewels In The Sun

God needs no electric power to work His miracles,
There within the garden He has no obstacles.

Coloured jewels of every hue were sparkling in the sun,
And trees were dressed for Christmas as the new day had begun!

Jewels that glistened wondrously, first blue then red, then green,
Each bare branch lit in splendour by the Hand of One unseen!

Sunshine glowing through the raindrops giving rainbow hue's,
What fairer sight to greet the day and chase away the 'blues'?

Such simple joys to ponder as the day brings forth its troubles.
Should we not bow in wonder as His grace and mercy doubles?

When eyes are opened fully to God's glories all around
To change the day that we might see His mysteries profound,

Bringing understanding of the things that we should know.
(There are so many mysteries that teach us the way to go!)

And we take so much for granted when we have no eyes to see
Beneath all nature's wonders unveiled for you and me.

Take time today to notice simple pleasures that inspire,
And maybe in the doing God will set your heart on fire!

****

Ride The Storm

Are we prepared for winter? Are we ready for each storm
That shadows life at any time, when everything goes wrong!

Is our storehouse overflowing for the time when we need aid?
Will our own strength be sufficient if we're lonely and afraid?

When Jesus lives within our heart then we are safe for sure,
His warmth and love enfolding brings peace that will endure.

With His loving cloak around us no winter storm can maim,
No fear of loneliness will harm, we'll ride the storm and claim

The help we need and we shall see that victory has been won,
By trusting Him and proving Him, to hear Him say 'Well done'.

POEMS

ELIZABETH TOMLINSON

Be Not Afraid

In the morning early
While lying on my bed
God gave to me
Words inside my head.

'Be not afraid' He said,
'I go before you always
However you may feel
On the good and bad days.'

'I will never fail you
Nor yet forsake,
So hold on in the pain
For I will undertake.'

'I've brought you through so much
In the years gone past
And My keeping power
Forever more will last.

In A Café

He looked at her,
Love shone from his face.
She was unaware
Sitting in her place
Of how wonderful
To him she did appear.
She was just a child
With her Daddy sitting there.
She was small and sweet
Out for a special treat,
With dolly by her side.
And dressed in pretty pink
She tucked into a scone
And enjoyed a chocolate drink.
Her Daddy, such a gentle man,
Spoke quietly with love
Reminding me of how
We have a Father up above
Who watches over us in awe,
And longs for us to know Him more.

For we to Him are precious,
Each and everyone,
So to draw us to Himself
He sent His only Son.
And one day He'll present us
At His Father's throne,
And Dad will be so pleased
To accept us as His own.

****

A Wonderful Sight.

There must have been five hundred or more.
They stood, stared at us not seen before.
They were so beautiful, a herd of deer
Yet their eyes were full of fear.
Then one by one they began to run.
So elegant, so agile,
We sat and watched awhile.
They dashed over the grass
Across the road pall mall
We stopped to let them pass,
Bucks, does and calves as well.

Dark clouds hovered above yet the sun was shining.
A rainbow appeared a gift of God's love!
'Twas a special time given by our Lord,
Then as we journeyed home it poured and poured!
'Twas as if for awhile we'd been in another world.
Just another touch of God's love unfurled!

SPRING POEMS

ELIZABETH TOMLINSON

Leaning on a Gate

Tiny new born lambs
Relaxing in the sun,
Such a lovely picture
Of life just begun.

Help us too to rest in You
In total trust and love,
For our Father God
Watches o'er us from above.

'Until There Was You'

I never saw the beauty of the flowers everywhere,
'Cos I didn't know their Maker and His love and care.
I never heard the music of the birds up in the sky,
Or their early morning singing perched in the branches high.
I never knew the wonder of our Lord's creation
'Til He came to me and I received His salvation!

So now the daffodils are trumpets of gold,
And the many little birds are marvels to behold.
And there is the sky above of many a delicate hue,
Pinks and blues, greys as well, since Lord I met You!
And every little animal specially lambs at play,
Cause me to praise You Lord on a lovely Spring day!

So dear Lord I praise You for opening up my eyes,
Now every day's a blessing, each one is God's surprise.

New Life

I looked up from my bed, saw blossoms on a tree,
All a gentle pink put there just for me!
To lift my spirit this early morn,
All God's handiwork to greet the dawn.
For months the branches had been bare,
Then suddenly new life was there.

Later on we strolled across a field so green.
Primroses and daisies were popping up
Where snow had been,
And little celandines were opening faces to the sun.
And once again I knew new life had begun.

SUMMER POEMS

ELIZABETH TOMLINSON

The Wagtail

Just a little wagtail
Special, perfectly made,
With black and white plumage
Beautifully arrayed.
Proudly he walked
Over a field of green,
A blessing that day,
A joy to be seen.
God reminded me
That we are tiny too,
Yet we are precious
Father God to You.
This world is so big,
We are so small,
'Tis a wonderful thing
That God cares for all.
He sees each bird
Each flower and tree,
So how much more
Does He keep you and me?

A Warm Summer Day

Sitting beneath the trees
Watching shadows
Dancing in the breeze,
Making patterns on the grass,
A delight to all that pass,
For outspread beneath my feet
Are designs, intricate, complete.
For the One who made the sea, the sky,
Made the trees to shelter you and I.

An Evening in June

A peacock butterfly
So perfect in design,
Stopped in front of me.
Looked so proud, so fine.
'Look at me' it seemed to say,
'I'm God's work of art'
Before it flew away
To make another start.
I knew the Master Artist
Had designed it so
To bless me that day
As onward I did go.
There's so much beauty
Everywhere, all around
For those with eyes to see,
Tiny flowers on the ground
Or fresh leaves upon a tree.
So as the sun shines down
Beneath a perfect sky of blue,
I relax dear Lord.
Give the glory all to You.

A Special Walk

We strolled hand in hand
Upon lovely warm sand.
I wished I could run,
Be a child, have some fun.
I couldn't run pell mell,
But I could marvel
At each tiny shell
At each tiny flower
Created in power.
So delicate, small,
There for us all.

I could feel the sea,
Sense its saltiness too.
Watch a seagull paddling
Beneath a sky of blue.
Many small details
I would miss
In this wide open space,
If I were a child
And decided to race.

A Beautiful Moment

A beautiful moment happened to me
As I sat in the sun podding many a pea!
A beautiful butterfly came, perched upon my chest,
A beautiful moment one of the best!
God's own handiwork intricate in design,
And for a moment this beauty was mine.
Maybe this butterfly needed a rest
And felt at ease relaxed upon my chest!

The Dragonfly

A dragonfly landed upon a stone
As if to pose for me alone!
'Twas a fleeting moment of delight
Before once again it took flight.

So beautiful in pattern green
I gazed in wonder and in awe,
For I had never seen
A dragonfly like this before.

As it flew between the reeds,
Wings so fragile and see through,
I praised God for His creation.
'Tis wonderful what He can do.

Starry Night

Thank You Lord that I'm in Your special care,
You will never leave my side, You always will be there!

I looked up at the stars You had flung into space
And almost felt Your Presence and saw Your smiling face!

For there in the silence in the darkness of the night,
As I relaxed alone my fears were put to flight!

For there in the darkness I felt Your light shine through,
And nothing that can happen can change my love for You!

Nothing past or present or that's yet to come
Can rob me of my future in my heavenly Home!

For no matter how I feel how downcast or sad,
My Father God is real, our true eternal Dad!

Who Could Not Believe?

Who could not believe when they see a humming bird?
And come to know the truth of God's everlasting word.
Who could not believe seeing the galaxy of stars above?
Or experience the dedication of a mother's love.

Who could not believe that life can still be worthwhile
On seeing a new born baby and sharing that first smile.
Who could not believe seeing the smallest flower?
So delicate and beautiful created by Almighty power!

Who could not believe when our needs are met?
As we realise afresh that God does not forget.
There are so many marvels but the greatest of them all
Is a heart redeemed by Jesus, God's free gift for us all.

Creator God!

As I write a poem some of me is in each line,
And as I look at God's Creation I see divine design.
So as we marvel more and more at His handiwork
His nature we can see
As we discover more and more we glimpse eternity.

For there's vibrant life just everywhere beneath the sea and in the
air,
In the bushes and the trees, floating and dancing in the breeze.
Under the earth and on the ground, God's character is all around.
In each rock pool, beneath each stone there's life, known to God
alone.

For He is the Master Artist, Sculptor and Poet too,
So if He is part of His Creation He is part of me and you!

AUTUMN POEMS

ELIZABETH TOMLINSON

An Autumn Walk

A canopy of colour
On autumn trees above,
A covering of blessing
Given with God's love.

Two dippers bathing
By the river side,
Bobbing up and down
With the flowing tide.

A sight we hadn't seen
For a long, long while,
Dippers having fun
Giving us a smile.

Seagulls on the water,
Squirrels dashing up a tree.
Wood pigeons all around
For those with eyes to see.

Just an autumn walk
On a dull November day,
Yet God surprised us
As we went on our way.

****

Autumn Glory

I stood and looked in wonder and awe
At so much glory ne'er seen before.

'Twas the autumn trees I did behold,
Their leaves of brown, yellow and gold.

All colours mingled a tapestry divine.
I stood amazed at this God of mine!

Others were gently fluttering down
In the welcome breeze around Richmond town.

The pathway before us was a carpet of leaves,
Truly God's blessing for one who believes!

Sadly the trees would soon be bare,
Yet underneath new life would appear.

So the seasons go on each with their own glory,
Ensuring the future of creations own story.

The Feather

A little feather floated to the ground,
It was as if a special treasure I had found.
So soft, in grey and white!
I picked it up, so fragile, a welcome sight
It blessed me as we strolled along
And put within a praising song,
That our mighty God,
Creator of the mountains tall
Could design with loving care
Each feather soft and small!

WINTER POEMS

ELIZABETH TOMLINSON

From My Window

There upon the lilac tree
Dainty little lights I see.
Transparent, sparkling
Blessing me.

Raindrops hanging like
Mini street lights,
God's adorning
Such lovely sights.

I sit by my window
On a damp January morn,
Yet I am still blessed
Though all looks forlorn.

So even on dark days
There's beauty around
Giving cause to praise
For God's gifts abound.

Another Special Moment

I walked past a window
On a wet windy day,
A child's smiling face
Delighted my way.
She looked full of mischief
And ready for fun,
With little eyes sparkling
She brought out the sun.

She was pleased to see me,
I hope I brightened her day,
As just one passer by
Who smiled back on their way.
A small simple thing,
An infectious smile,
Can bless and uplift
Make life worthwhile.

8164500R00059

Printed in Great Britain
by Amazon.co.uk, Ltd.,
Marston Gate.